Energy

Sector

Erik Johnson
Copyright © 2020 FYMM

All rights reserved.

ISBN:

9798586614223

BOOK TITLE

CONTENTS

1	Kinder Morgan	1
2	Magellan Midstream Partners	3
3	Sunoco	6
4	Chevron Corp	11
5	Exxon Mobil	19
6	Eni SpA	24
7	Valero Energy Corp	28
8	Total	32
9	Royal Dutch Shell	36
10	3M	40

terminals. They Transport all types of gases and oil products.

As we can see they have a massive network expanding the united states. The great thing about this company is it dividends. And a high institutional ownership. Over the last 5 years insiders have been buying about 1,511,403 shares per year.

1 KINDER MORGAN

Kinder Morgan has one of the largest energy infrastructure United States. They have an impressive 83,000 miles of pipelines and 147

2 MAGELLAN MIDSTREAM PARTNERS

This is a publicly traded partnership that primarily transports stores and distributes refined petroleum products based in Oklahoma. in

2004 they made a huge purchase from Shell which included three thousand miles of refined product pipelines as long as Terminals and storage capacity. Today Magellan has 9800 miles of refined products pipeline system with over 54 connected terminal in 25 independent terminals not connected to the pipelines they also have to Marine storage terminals .

The company also has over 2,000 200 miles of crude oil pipelines and storage facilities with a capacity of 37 million barrels of which 25 million are already under contract. The partnership owns the longest refined petroleum products pipeline system in the country with access to over 50% of the United States refining capacity with having such access and importance in the gasoline fuel and crude oil business they've able to pee healthy consistent dividend which has increased 683% since their IPO

3 SUNOCO

Sunoco:

is a chain of convenience stores and Retail fuel sites so each Sunoco is company owned and operated. Not only do they own approximately 9200 convenience stores and gas stations around the United States they also are one of the largest wholesale distributions of motor fuels to other convenience stores and other gas stations. To achieve this success the company is broken into three different sections Sunoco LP, Sunoco race fuels, And Sunoco.

Sunoco:

Sonoco proper is the 9200 different gas stations and Retail stations around the United States. Sunoco ultratech significantly exceeds the

USA Environmental Protection agency's gasoline detergent standards and for over a hundred years sunoco's gasoline has been known for its high quality.

Sunoco LP:

Sunoco LP is the largest fuel distributor in the United States; they distribute their petroleum products to convenience stores, independent dealers and commercial customers in more than 33 States. Sunoco LP owns and operates 13 fuel terminals across the United States.

Sunoco race fuels:

Racing has been in sunoco's blood since the early 50s when they first Blended their high octane fuels. In 2004 Sunoco became the official fuel of NASCAR Grand Am and ARCA sanctioned racing. In 2009 Sunoco became the official fuel of AMA Pro road racing. In 2011 Sunoco became the official fuel for Izod IndyCar and Indy lights series racing. in 2015 became the official fuel of the NHRA drag racing

4 CHEVRON CORP

Chevron Corporation.

Chevron's expertise is in a range of different products and services. They are in Exploration and production, refining, Transportation, chemicals and additives Chevron lubricants, products and services, and supply & Trading.

Exploration and production:

There is heavy oil, deep-water, liquefied Natural Gas, regular oil natural gas, shell/tight resources. They're up sting operations span the globe they have operations in Africa asia-pacific Eurasia Europe Latin America the Middle East and North America.

Refining:

Seven of Chevron's refineries make up more than 95% of the total crude refining capacity; the five core refineries are in Singapore Thailand South Korea Richmond and El Segundo California. They sell their refined products under the names Chevron, Texaco, and caltex brands they also recently completed major upgrades in several their refinery Implementing a loss prevention system at all the facilities.

Transportation:

In this department of Chevron they have two different companies they have Chevron pipeline company and Chevron Shipping Company Chevron pipeline company transports the Natural Gas the liquefied Natural Gas carbon dioxide petrochemicals crude oil and Chevron Shipping Company manages a fleet of vessels to ship the crude a staggering and commendable feed Chevron Fleet travels approximately 55 trips around the world each year around 1.4 million miles.

Chemicals and additives:

Chevron chemical and additives company is a 50/50 joint venture with Phillips Chemical Company their products are used to make food packaging cleaner fuels biodegradable solvents lubricant additives. they're headquartered in The Woodlands Texas and they employ over 5,000 employees across 30 different regions and countries.

Chevron lubricants:

Chevron lubricants has over 30 years of experience manufacturing premium oils. they create lubricants for commercial transportation, passenger vehicles, industrial and off road equipment, and Marine lubricants

Products and services:

Their brands are Chevron which is committed to advance innovation and high quality care for your car Texaco with over A Century of delivering high performance fuel and Caltex all around the world customers can meet their needs without compromise

Supply & Trading:

Chevron Supply & Trading is the critical link between Upstream, Downstream, and the chemical companies. they provide the much-needed support for the crude and natural gas production. they buy, sel,l and transport all major grades of crude oil by doing this it secures the best prices for Chevron

Upstream production. the product and Supply trading manages Global Supply and logistics for feedstocks fuels refined products and all other of the marketed products

5 EXXON MOBIL

Exxon Mobil

they are one of the largest publicly traded energy providers and chemical manufacturers. Worldwide ExxonMobil markets fuels and lubricants under these Iconic Brands; Esso, Exxon, Mobil, and ExxonMobil chemical.

Esso:

Esso was originally the Standard Oil of New Jersey following the Standard Oil breakup in 1972 in the United States the name was largely replaced by Exxon however around the world Esso is still a prominent name. During the racial segregation years in the United States the SOS franchises gave out the Negro motorist green book an international travel guide for Negroes during the time of segregation outlining safe routes for them to take.

Mobil:

In 1999 Exxon and Mobil joined together to bring ExxonMobil It is the same company however mobile is the primary retail gasoline brand in California, New York, New England, the great lakes and the Midwest you will also see Mobile gasoline stations in Australia, Canada, Colombia, Egypt, Guam,

Japan, Malaysia, Mexico, New Zealand and Nigeria.

Exxon:

Exxon the flagship brand creates synthetic blend of oil and gasoline to increase fuel economy so you can go more miles for every tank took protect your engine to burn cleaner and reduce emissions and enhance power coming from an improved engine performance.

ExxonMobil chemical:

ExxonMobil chemical is one of the largest chemical companies in the world more than 90% of the company's chemical capacity is integrated with ExxonMobil refineries or natural gas processing pants they also have manufacturing capacity in every major region of the world.

6 ENI SPA

Eni SpA:

is Global Energy company with the goal to become a leader in the production and sale of decarbonized products. With

Partnerships in Italy and around the world allows Eni SpA to develop solar wind and wave power. Vapor check by 2050 gas will account for 85% of Upstream production .

Eni SpA Cease hydrogen as the next worldwide solution for meeting climate challenges their belief comes from the qualities of energy hydrogen creates without creating CO_2 emissions during combustion. hydrogen is also the simplest and most abundant element on Earth ninety-eight percent of hydrogen today comes from fossil fuels they are the largest producer and consumer of hydrogen in Italy Today hydrogen is usually used for feedstock as well as biorefineries in Venice and Gala for the production of hydrotreated vegetable oil biofuels

An Italy-Based Company Operating In Exploration, Development And Production Of Hydrocarbons, In The Supply And Marketing Of Gas,

Liquefied Natural Gas (LNG) And Power.

They Look To Be Transitioning To Alternative Solar Energy

Its Gas & Power Segment Engages In Supply, Trading And Marketing Of Gas, LNG And Electricity, International Gas Transport Activities And Commodity Trading And Derivatives. So Be Careful Their Dividend Could Fluctuate . This Is A Long Term Play On Alternative Energy And LNG

7 VALERO ENERGY CORP

Valero:

Throughout the United States and Canada Valero owns and operates 15 different refineries 11 ethanol plants and a 50 megawatt wind farm they're also one of the largest retail operators with close to 6800 retail stations. Valero Can be categorized into three segments refining, ethanol, and renewable diesel.

Refining:

Valero acquires 2.2 million barrels of crude oil a day from suppliers this is shipped through pipe rail trucks and ships the crude is been stored in their refineries with a capacity of 26.2 million barrels .

Ethanol:

Valero is known to use every kernel of the corn to produce ethanol which is a clean-burning high-octane renewable fuel the green dry or modified would stay use as high-value feed for cattle swine and poultry and Fuel and feed grade corn oil to make Renewable Diesel Fuel and livestock feed.They share 20% of the US ethanol exports in 2019 they're the second largest corn ethanol producer and they produce 1.7 billion gallons per year

.

Renewable diesel:

Diamond green diesel renewable Refinery is in Norco Louisiana and is a joint venture with darling ingredients. Producing over 275 million gallons per year they produce Diesel from animal fats, used cooking oil, and inedible corn.

8 TOTAL

Total ,

Total is a major energy player food produces and supplies oil natural gas and low-carbon electricity they are active in 130 + countries with over a hundred thousand employees. their Origins date back to 1924. They service over 8 million customers a day through their gas stations they are also the second largest liquefied natural gas company.

As of December 2014 total had a 903 subsidiaries. They are involved in 23 projects of exploration and production in Africa Asia Europe North America South America and Russia.

They are the number one distributor of biofuels in Europe 2.5 million metric tons of biofuels blended into gasoline and diesel in 2019. They are also heavily invested in solar energy total solar will help install panels on roofs of Industrial and Commercial buildings or parking lots and canopies through SunPower a leading manufacturer of high-efficiency photovoltaic cells through total Eren they build and operate solar power plants and wind farms primarily in asia-pacific Africa and Latin America.

9 ROYAL DUTCH SHELL

Royal Dutch Shell.

the brand encompasses two complementary but distinct business units through an established energy marketing and trading business service in Europe the Americas Asia Australia that she'll energy brand now extends into residential sector with home energy launch in Great Britain. Royal Dutch Shell is the fifth largest company in the world measured by 2020 revenues and the largest in Europe. they are integrated in every active area of oil and gas industry including exploration production refining transport distribution in marketing petrochemicals power generation and trading it also has activities in renewable energy biofuels wind hydrogen and energy kite systems.

they have operations in 70 countries producing 3 million barrels a day with 44000 service stations worldwide. shell began drilling for oil in Africa during the 1950's they still operate in the Upstream oil sector in Algeria Cameroon Egypt Gabon Ghana Libya Morocco Nigeria South Africa and Tunisia in the downstream sector there in 16 other countries. They also have a very strong presence in Asia with operations in India Singapore the Philippines Brunei Malaysia Hong Kong and China.

10 BP

BP :

BP is the global brand which name is often Appears on platforms, refineries, ships, Corporate Office,s wind farms, research facilities, and Retail service stations. As the BP brand logo appears everywhere in our daily lives it is less well-known of the other companies BP owns such as Castrol lubricants, Aral, AMPM, Amoco, Wild Bean Cafe

Castrol lubricants:

In 2002 BP acquired Castrol lubricants today their products are sold in 150 companies and They are preferred partner for VW, Audi, BMW, and Komatsu. While using Castrol lubricants their sponsored Motorsports teams have broken the speed record more than 20 times.

Aral:

Over 2.5 million people visit Aral service station Everyday making it one of Germany's leading fuel retail brands. They are also Germany's third largest fast food retailer they consistently win Awards in Germany as the most trusted fuel.

AMPM:

If you live on the west coast of the United States then ampm is a part of your daily life they are across five states from Southern California to northern Oregon with 950 Outlets they are known for their quality food and their soft drinks. many ampm's are attached to BP fuel stations.

Amoco:

Officially known as Standard Oil Indiana by 1912 they became the largest natural gas producer in North America. in October 2017 BP announced the reintroduction of Amoco to the United States as a fuel retailer. in 1998 is when BP and Amoco merged But in 2001 BP Amoco changed Simply BP.

Wild Bean Cafe:

Many of these branches are attached to BP connect fuel stations with offering freshly baked goods and Barista prepared coffees although you will not see these in the United States you will see them in the UK, Europe, Australia, South Africa, China, and Russia.

www.ingramcontent.com/pod-product-compliance
Lightning Source LLC
Chambersburg PA
CBHW070900220526
45466CB00005B/2059